THE SMASHING SAXONS

TERRY DEARY

Illustrated by Martin Brown

Brought to you by

The Daily Telegraph

For George Barron, with thanks

This edition is produced for The Daily Telegraph

Scholastic Children's Books, Euston House, 24 Eversholt Street, London, NW1 1DB

For promotional use only. Not for resale

Selling or purchasing this book on the internet or otherwise may constitute a criminal offence.

First published in the UK by Scholastic Ltd, 2000

ISBN 1 4071 0274 5

Typeset by M Rules
Printed and bound by Norhaven Paperback A/S, Denmark

Contents

Introduction

History can be horrible. Especially those history lessons where the teacher asks impossible questions. You know the sort of thing …

Forget all the confusing stuff teachers try to tell you …

'Saxon' was a name the Welsh, the Scots and the Irish called all the strangers who moved into England when the Romans left. Just tell your teacher: 'It was never that simple. Let's just use the word "Saxon" the way they meant it. Saxons were the people who invaded the place we now call England.'

And don't worry … there is an escape from the terrible tortures of teachers asking questions.

It's time for pupil power and for biting back! Now, with the help of a *Horrible Histories* book, you can turn the tables on teachers. Now *you* can ask the questions!

Knowledge is power, see? Now you can find out fascinating facts, like what a whip made from the skin of a dolphin would be used for, and then test your teacher.

By the time you've finished the teacher may need that whip. Why? Read on …

Timeline

410 After 300 years the Romans in Britain go back to Rome. The Brits have to fight off powerful Picts, savage Scots and invading Irish raiders.

449 The Brits hire a couple of bothersome Saxon brothers from Jutland, Hengest and Horsa, to fight for them. H & H like it so much they decided to stay, batter the Brits and settle. There's gratitude for you!

460s The Brits fight back against the Saxons under a leader called Ambrosius and about twenty years later a warrior called Arthur takes over. That's not the legendary bloke with a round table. This King Arthur was probably the last great Roman British leader.

491 The Saxon leader Aelle (call him 'Ella') becomes the first ruler of a South Saxon kingdom. He attacks British defenders at the old Roman fortress in Pevensey and massacres the lot of them.

511 Brit hero King Arthur dies (probably) at the battle of Camlann. The Brits will struggle hopelessly now he's gone.

597 Christian missionaries arrive from Rome and Saxons are

converted – mostly. (Some go back to being pagans later. Maybe it's more fun.)

600s The Saxons gradually take over the land we now call England with the Northumbrian kingdom in the north, the Mercians in the middle, the Anglians in the East and the kingdom of Wessex in the south. Very neat, very cosy.

787 Mercian leader King Offa is so powerful he can organize the digging of a 20-metre-wide ditch between England and Wales, 169 miles (270 km) long to keep the wild Welsh away. His ditch is known as Offa's Dyke.

793 The Vikings are coming from Norway. Bad news for savaged Saxons and massacred monks. These are just raids – later they'll be back to stay.

871 Alfred the Great becomes king of Wessex and defeats and drives back the vicious Vikings from the south of England. But they don't go home. They stay in the north and the east. Alfie may be 'Great' but he hasn't vanquished the Vikings really.

924 Alf's grandson, Athelstan, avoids a plot to blind him and becomes king. He's a real 'great'

8

even though he's usually forgotten. He's the man to sort out the Vikings, not to mention the Welsh and the Scots. Wessex are winners! Britain is a single Saxon country for the first time. But not for long …

937 The Welsh, Scots, Irish and Vikings all gang up to rebel and destroy Athelstan. He and his Saxons beat them in a bloody battle at Brunanburh – probably in Yorkshire. **939** Athelstan dies. Guess what? The Vikings are back, led by Olaf Guthfrithsson who takes over as king in the north. He means trouble. **978** Saxon King Edward the Martyr is murdered. Ethelred the Unready (his step-brother) takes the crown. But did Eth have something to do with the death? Eth tries to pay the Vikings to go away – giving them gold weighing 10,000 kilos in 991 – so they keep coming back! Who can blame them? **1002** King Ethelred organizes a massacre of the Viking settlers – the women and children and the defenceless farmers, because they don't fight back! But the Viking warriors will avenge them. **1012** Now poor old Eth gives the greedy Vikings 20,000 kilos of gold

to go away. It does him (and the English) no good because …

1013 Ethelred is driven off the throne and replaced by invading Viking Sweyn. Eth runs off to Normandy till Sweyn dies. Eth tries a bit of a comeback but then Sweyn's son Cnut returns and sees him off.

1042 Edward the Confessor becomes king. He gets a bit too friendly with the Normans.

1066 …and that's that! Last Saxon king, Harold, is defeated by William the Conqueror and his Normans.

The Saxon start

Battering the Brits

Have you ever noticed how school books *tell* you things but they never seem to answer the questions you want to ask. But this is a *Horrible Histories* book, so now's your chance to quiz the author. Well? What are you waiting for?

WHO WERE THESE SAXON PEOPLE?

Well they came from North Germany and invaded Britain from about AD 300 onwards. They liked it so much they stayed.

SO WHAT WAS WRONG WITH NORTH GERMANY THEN?

A lot of them lived on little islands surrounded by marsh or sea. Terrible farming land, so they went off and pinched someone else's.

DID NO ONE TRY TO STOP THEM?

Of course they did! The Romans who ran Britain stopped them. Then, when the Romans left, the Brits tried to stop them.

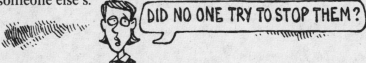

BUT THE SAXONS WON?

They drove the Brits west into Wales and Cornwall. Then the Vikings came across and tried to push the Saxons out.

SERVES THEM RIGHT! SO WHY ISN'T ENGLAND CALLED SAXONLAND?

Just one of those things. It was the Welsh and the Scots and the Irish who called them Saxons. By about 800, the Saxons were calling themselves 'Anglisc' – their spelling wasn't as good as yours.

OK, WHERE DID THE SAXONS GO?

Nowhere. They stayed in Britain. But in 1066 the Normans came across and took control. The Normans became the rulers and the Saxons became the peasants. Today's British people are a mixture of Saxon and Norman and lots of others.

SO WHAT KIND OF PEOPLE WERE THESE SAXONS?

That would take a whole book to answer.

BOOKS ARE BORING!

Horrible Histories aren't.

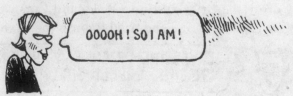

SO WHERE CAN I FIND A HORRIBLE HISTORY OF THE SAXONS?

You're reading it, stupid!

OOOOH! SO I AM!

Horrible Hengest

In the 420s the Brits were led by Vortigern.

HERE! I SAY, YOU CHAPS! THAT WASN'T MY *NAME* YOU KNOW! VORTIGERN WAS MY *TITLE* AND IT MEANS 'GREAT KING'. JOLLY GOOD TITLE TOO!

Vortigern led the Brits from about AD 425 till 450. He organized the Brits after the Roman armies left and his real name may have been Vitalinus – which sounds a bit like a medicine.

But Vortigern had problems, as we know from a horrible history written by a priest and historian called Gildas, who was writing almost a hundred years after Vortigern ruled.

> **T**he feathered flight of a rumour reached the ears of everyone in south Britain. Their old enemies from the north were on their way. They weren't coming to raid but to rule the country from end to end. But before they could defend themselves they rushed down that wide road that leads to death. A deadly plague killed so many and so quickly that there weren't enough left alive to bury the dead ...

What did the Brits do when peppered by plague and Picts?

PANIC! THOSE PICT RUFFIANS ARE COMING AND THERE AREN'T ENOUGH BRIT BOYS LEFT TO FIGHT THEM OFF. PICTS ARE TERRIBLE PEOPLE! THEY'LL KILL YOU, OR WORSE ... MAKE YOU EAT HAGGIS! YEUCH!

DEATH OR HAGGIS? TAKE YOUR PICT!

DEFINITELY DEATH

So what did Vortigern do? Gildas said Vortigern's council 'went blind'. What he *meant* was they couldn't see how stupid their actions were ...

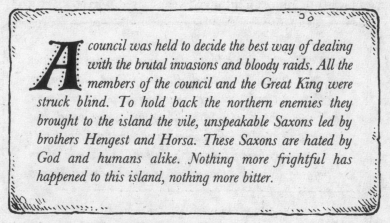

A council was held to decide the best way of dealing with the brutal invasions and bloody raids. All the members of the council and the Great King were struck blind. To hold back the northern enemies they brought to the island the vile, unspeakable Saxons led by brothers Hengest and Horsa. These Saxons are hated by God and humans alike. Nothing more frightful has happened to this island, nothing more bitter.

Do you get the feeling that Gildas didn't like the Saxons?

He went on to curse Vortigern and the council …

What utter blindness of their wits. What raw, hopeless stupidity!

Sounds a bit like my teacher when he read my history homework!

Anyway, Vortigern paid the warrior-bullies Hengest and Horsa to fight for him …

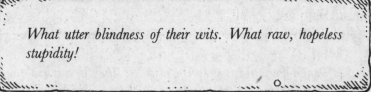

AND THE BOYS DONE WELL

…but then the Saxon visitors turned nasty and demanded a lump of Brit land for themselves. One hundred years later, Gildas was still furious at Vortigern's stupidity …

Vortigern's council invited an enemy under their own roof that they feared more than death. These Saxons fixed their claws on the eastern coast, as if they planned to defend it. When they were settled they invited friends to join them. For a long time the Britons gave them supplies to 'shut the dog's mouth'.

But the Saxon 'dogs' were hungry. The more they got the more they wanted and they were ready to fight for it.

Vortigern's plan worked for a little while and the Picts and Irish were held back. The *Kentish Chronicle* history makes it sound pathetic …

> *The Saxon barbarians grew in number. They demanded the food and clothing that Vortigern promised but the Britons said, 'We cannot feed and clothe you, for your numbers are grown. Go away, for we do not need your help.'*

Imagine being in the Brits' position. You ask the school bully to help you. He turns on you and demands your school dinner money. And you say, 'Go away, for I do not need your help!' Think it would work?

Hah! No way. And it didn't work for the Britons. But then another Roman Briton called Ambrosius rebelled against Vortigern. Who did Vortigern turn to for help to fight Ambrosius?

MY BRAVE SAXON CHUMS OF COURSE. NATURALLY OLD HENGEST TOLD ME HE DIDN'T HAVE ENOUGH FIGHTING FELLOWS TO BATTLE AGAINST ALL OF AMBROSIUS' AWFUL MEN. HE WANTED TO FETCH ANOTHER TWENTY BOATLOADS OF HIS SAXON MATES ACROSS

Hengest didn't just bring more warriors. He brought a secret weapon: his daughter! The old historian describes what happened next ...

In one of the ships was Hengest's daughter, a very beautiful girl. Hengest arranged a feast for Vortigern and his soldiers. They got very drunk and the Devil entered into Vortigern's heart, making him fall in love with the girl. He asked Hengest for her hand in marriage and said, 'I will give anything you want in return – even half my kingdom!'

Of course it wasn't Vortigern's kingdom to give away! The land belonged to the dukes who ruled each county. But Vortigern gave Hengest the county of Kent – without even asking the Kent lord Gwyrangon.

In around AD 449, from his new base in Kent, Hengest was ready to take over Britain and he didn't care how much blood was spilled. Gildas said ...

All the great towns fell to the Saxon battering rams. Bishops, priests and people were all chopped down together while swords flashed and flames crackled. It was horrible to see the stones of towers thrown down to mix with pieces of human bodies. Broken altars were covered with a purple crust of clotted blood. There was no burial except under ruins and bodies were eaten by the birds and beasts.

Horrible history! But a bit over the top. Modern historians don't think the Saxon rebellion was all that bloody and violent.

Anyway, the Brits fought back ...

I SENT MY OWN SON, VORTEMIR, OFF TO FIGHT OLD HENGEST. YOU KNOW, HE WHIPPED THE SAXONS LIKE DOGS AND KILLED OLD HENGEST'S BROTHER HORSA. I THINK THE SAVAGE SAXONS GOT MY MESSAGE: YOU DON'T MESS WITH VORTIGERN

Then young Vortemir was killed. The Saxons came back with a really 'vile, unspeakable' plot. If Vortigern had left a diary it might have looked something like this ...

24th August, St Bartholomew's Day, AD 456

Oh dear!
Oh dear, oh dear!
Oh dear, oh dear, oh dear!
Those frightfully nice Saxon chappies have turned out to be simply... well, frightful. It was bad enough their killing poor little Vortemir but now they've turned nasty.

That Hengest blokee (who smells a little, to be honest) invited us over to talk about peace and one thought it was a jolly good idea, don't you know. After all, I'm married to his lovely daughter, so he wouldn't harm me. 'Bring along your top generals, no weapons though,' he said. 'We'll have a bit of a party — some ale, a few nibbles and a jolly sing song!' It sounded just like the good old days when the Saxon blokes first came over.

In fact it all sounded jolly jolly. 'When would you like us to come over?' one asked.

'Saint Bartholomew's Eve — seven thirty for eight,' he said.

'Topping!' one replied. 'See you then, old boy.' Oh, dear, oh, dear. The clue was there, wasn't it? Saint Bartholomew was that missionary chappie who went to Africa to convert the pagans. They skinned him alive and chopped his head off. So one ought to have guessed that it wasn't a good evening to meet the jolly old pagan enemy.

Sure enough I arrived with all the top chaps in Britain — my best warriors, best ministers and the best bishops. What did the savage Saxons do? Why they sat us down at the tables, waited till we were munching on the jolly old nibbles and then Hengest cried out, 'Saxons! Draw your knives!' They jolly well drew their dirty great knives that they'd hidden in their boots! Not very sporting. In fact it's cheating, don't you think?

Chop! Chop! Chop! It was over in seconds — well, actually we didn't have any seconds. They killed the chaps while they were eating their firsts! Blood all over the tables. Blood all over the rushes on the floor. Someone's going to have a sticky, messy, job cleaning that up one can jolly well tell you! The only one they left alive was me. One has to go back and tell the British

chaps that 'Hengest rules OK!' Since
one has lost all one's top chappies one
doesn't have a lot of choice, does one?

I'm a prisoner and I had to give horrible
Hengest quite a lot of land just to spare
my life.
Oh dear!
Oh dear, oh dear!
Oh dear, oh dear, oh dear!

What happened to Vortigern? He survived but was hated
by everyone. In the end …

*Vortigern wandered from place to place till his heart broke
and he died without honour.*

Gildas the writer was trying to explain what a dreadful
place Britain was and how it had been better in the good old
Roman days. Maybe he made the Saxon rebellion sound
worse than it was. Archaeologists have dug on a lot of Saxon
and British sites and they can't find much proof that this
violent rebellion ever happened.

But, violent or peaceful, the Saxons had arrived and they
meant to stay.

21

Superstitious Saxons

The Dark Ages are a bit of a mystery to us – that's how they got their name. But they were also really dark! After the sun set there were no streetlights to show the way. Only moonlight, starlight and some whacking great scary shadows.

So it's no wonder the Saxons believed all sorts of weird and horrible things went on in those shadows. Devils and demons lurked there, ready to snatch your soul and carry it off to Hell!

EVEN THOUGH I SAY IT MYSELF, IF THERE'S ONE THING I DO RATHER WELL, IT'S LURK

You believed in charms and spells to protect you. You became superstitious – especially about how you buried your dead.

Dead losses

In the early days, before they became Christian, the Saxons would sometimes bury a servant with his (or her) dead master. The servant would then be able to serve the master in the afterlife. But the horrible historical fact is the servant was often buried alive! They were thrown into the open grave, a heavy stone may have been thrown on top to keep them down and then they were covered with soil.

If it wasn't a servant then it was some poor woman, buried alive to keep the man company in the afterlife – cook his dinner, wash his clothes and polish his sword. It seems that even in the afterlife men were hopeless!

Even dogs were sacrificed to go with their masters to the afterlife. What would dogs *do* there? Are there any trees for pees in heaven?

The Saxons brought a lot of their funeral habits with them from Europe. Then, in AD 597 St Augustine arrived in southern England to convert the Saxons to Christianity. When the Saxons became Christian there was a mixture of old customs and new ones ... and some customs you wouldn't want to happen to your worst enemy or even your history teacher ...

A pane in the ash

Saxons were worried about the ghosts of the dead coming back to haunt them.

Would you worry about your dead Auntie Ethelburga coming back to haunt you? Then here are a few helpful early-Saxon hints ...

1 Cremate her. When early Saxons cremated a dead friend they would place the ashes in a small jar or urn. Then they would leave a small window in the jar. Why? So the spirit could come and go and not make trouble if it found its ashes trapped in a sealed container.

MIND YOU, WINDOWS DO HAVE THEIR DISADVANTAGES

I CAN SEEEEE YOU!

2 Cut her head off. The living dead find it a bit hard to haunt without a head. They wouldn't even find their way out of the burial yard. So lop off their dead head and save yourself from a haunting.

3 Give her some company. Sometimes there were the ashes of more than one person in a pot. Auntie Ethelburga will be so busy gossiping to her powdered pal that she'll forget to haunt you.

4 Give her some treasure. The dead are happy if they are buried with some of their precious possessions. Women could be buried with jewellery like dress fasteners. A man might be buried with a sword or throwing spear. (He's bound to be a dead shot.)

5 Burn crops. Garlic keeps vampires away, they say, and the Saxons believed burning crops kept ghosts away. (Do *not* try this with your breakfast cornflakes. Especially after your mum's poured milk over them). This useful trick was banned by boring Archbishop Theodore in AD 672.

WHY WASTE WORTHWHILE WHEAT WHEN WE WANT WICKEDNESS WITHDRAWN?

It's just as well the Saxons had these ghost-busting ideas because there were a lot of dead people around. Half of them were dead before they reached 25 years old and not many of the rest reached 40.

Good god

When the Saxons first came to Britain they were 'pagans' – they worshipped German gods like ...

GODS

Name: Tiw

Day to remember: Tuesday named after him.

Top job: God of 'Justice'.

Foul fact: He allowed himself to be used as the bait to trap a monstrous wolf. The wolf bit his hand off. Don't try this at home. (Maybe he should also be the god of stupidity.)

Name: Woden
Day to remember: Wednesday named after him.
Top job: The top god and god of poets.
Foul fact: He owned an eight-legged horse (must have cost a fortune in horse-shoes) that could fly through the air. He swapped one of his eyes for wisdom – don't try this at school.

Name: Thunor
Day to remember: Thursday named after him.
Top job: God of thunder.
Foul fact: Had a magic throwing hammer that came back to him like a boomerang. (Don't try this in the park.) Incredibly strong but has so far failed to smash the skull of the serpent of evil. He'll do it at Ragnarok – that's the end of the worlds of gods and humans.

Name: Frigg
Day to remember: Friday named after her.
Top job: Woden's wife – goddess of marriage.
Foul fact: She didn't lose an eye or a hand but she did lose her son, Balder, who was killed with the only thing that could harm him – mistletoe. (So watch what you stand under next Christmas!)

Although the Saxons later converted to being Christians they kept bits of their old religion in their religious ceremonies. They were a mixture of Christian and pagan – maybe they believed the Christian God and the pagan gods would work together for better effect!

Foul fields

Do you have a field that has been cursed? Maybe a school football field where you always seem to lose? Why not get your head teacher to try this ancient Saxon cure?

FIRST CUT FOUR SQUARES OF TURF FROM EACH CORNER OF THE FIELD. WATCH OUT FOR THOSE WORMS!

MIX OIL, HONEY, YEAST, MILK, SAWDUST AND HOLY WATER. THEN SPRINKLE THE MIXTURE ON TO THE UNDERSIDE OF THE TURF - GIVE THOSE WORMS A BATH

YUM!

SEND FOR YOUR PRIEST WHO MUST MAKE FOUR CROSSES FROM POPLAR WOOD-OR A COUPLE OF LOLLY STICKS MAY DO THE TRICK

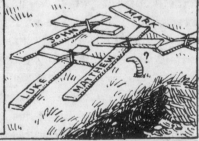

WRITE A NAME ON EACH: MATTHEW, MARK, LUKE AND JOHN. PLACE THE CROSSES IN THE HOLES LEFT WHERE YOU REMOVED THE TURF AND HOPE THE WORMS AREN'T TOO CROSS

JOHN MARK LUKE MATTHEW ?

THE PRIEST MUST THEN BOW NINE TIMES TO THE EAST AND TURN NINE TIMES CLOCKWISE BEFORE PUTTING THE TURFS BACK. BET THE WORMS ARE GLAD TO BE HOME

'ALTOGETHER, CHANT THIS SPELL:
'ERCE, ERCE, ERCE, MOTHER OF
 EARTH,
MAY THE ALMIGHTY ETERNAL
 LORD GRANT THEE
FIELDS GROWING AND SPRINGING
FRUITFUL AND STRENGTH-GIVING'

If all that doesn't make you win you could always try an ancient pagan practice and sacrifice the referee.

Did you know ... ?
Even though the historian Saint Bede was a good Christian, and believed in the power of God, he also believed a lot of the superstitions of the Saxon people – and so did most of the Christians who lived at the time. He believed that God sent messages to people on earth through his miracles ... and also through strange signs.

In the year 729 Bede reported that there were two comets seen in the skies. He said this was a heavenly sign that a disaster was going to happen. In fact an army from Asia attacked France and caused a lot of death and destruction to Christians there.

In 734 there were reports that the moon turned the colour of blood and blood rained down from the skies – shortly afterwards Bede died!

THIS IS A BAD SIGN!

YORK
this way
or maybe
← this way

What other odd ideas did the Saxons have ... ?

Wacky weather wisdom

The Saxons watched out for signs for their weather forecasts – but signs didn't just foretell the weather! What did these signs mean?

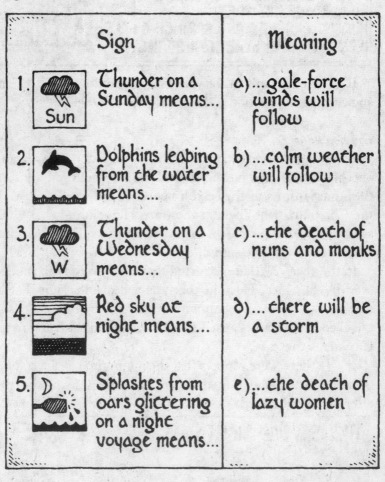

Sign	Meaning
1. Thunder on a Sunday means...	a)...gale-force winds will follow
2. Dolphins leaping from the water means...	b)...calm weather will follow
3. Thunder on a Wednesday means...	c)...the death of nuns and monks
4. Red sky at night means...	d)...there will be a storm
5. Splashes from oars glittering on a night voyage means...	e)...the death of lazy women

Answers: 1c); 2a); 3e); 4b); 5d).

30

Sutton who?

In 1939 some archaeologists began digging into a Saxon burial mound. It was at a place called Sutton Hoo, not far from the town of Ipswich in East Anglia, and the site turned out to be a great discovery.

But sixty years later no one can quite agree what they uncovered. It was a 24 metre wooden ship from around the year AD 600, buried with treasure in memory of a great person. There were over 40 gold items and a great silver dish. Most historians agree on that ... but not much else. For example, there was an iron stand found in the grave. They argue it was either ...

- a torch holder
- a standard (sort of a flag-pole) for soldiers to follow
- or a rack to show off the scalps of dead enemies!

HAS ANYONE SEEN MY SPEAR FRAME?

But that's not all historians disagree about …

Was there ever a body in the boat?

Archaeologists and scientists looked at soil samples and grave goods for forty years and couldn't agree. Then, in 1979, they decided to look at the notes made by the first diggers. And they made an amazing discovery. There in the notes was one line no one had noticed before ...

Complete set of iron coffin fittings arranged in a rectangle

There *had* been a coffin after all! So it's pretty certain there was a body in the grave! What happened to these important clues, the coffin fittings?

Hoo knows? They are missing.

Did you know ... ?

Some Saxon helmets had a wild pig on top. No! Not a real one, dummy. A little metal model.

WHY DID SAXON HELMETS HAVE PIGS ON?

I'm glad you asked me that.

The pig was sacred to the god of peace, Frey, and the goddess of battle and death, his sister Freyja. The pig was a good luck sign!

Next time you have a school exam or a SAT test, why not try wearing a wild pig on your head?

WILL A SLICE OF BACON BRING ME A SLICE OF LUCK?

Awesome Arthur

The years from about AD 450 till around 500 were the darkest years of the Dark Ages.

Battered Brits bite back

Luckily the priest Gildas gives us a horrible historical idea of what it was like then for the poor old Brits ...

> *Some of the wretched British were caught in the hills and slaughtered in heaps. Some gave themselves up as slaves. Some hid in the thick forests and the cliffs, terrified, until the savage Saxon raiders went home again.*

The Saxons were battering the Brits, but some Brits started fighting back. They wanted a Britain the way it was in the old Roman days of eighty years before. One leader managed to win forty years of peace. He was called 'the last Roman' and his name was Arthur.

Five hundred years after Arthur died his name was remembered and storytellers came up with some great tales of Arthur's deeds. In a word they were bosh. In four words they were total and utter bosh. Any historian will tell you ...

Happy History for Cute Kids

- King Arthur pulled a magical sword from a stone. *Bosh!*

- Arthur was given his war sword, Excalibur, by the Lady of the Lake. *Tosh!*

- Arthur gathered his knights at a round table at the wonderful palace of Camelot. *Piffle!*

- Arthur and his knights fought against evil in their shining armour. *Twaddle!*

- Arthur was betrayed by the wicked Mordred and beaten in battle. *Tommyrot!*

- Now Arthur is lying asleep and he will awaken and return when Britain is in danger. *Tripe!*

The truth is there are very few clues as to who Arthur was, what he did, or even where he lived and fought. A monk called Nennius wrote of twelve battles that Arthur fought in.

The twelfth battle was on Badon Hill where 960 men fell in one day from one attack by Arthur. No one killed them but he alone.

Arthur killed 960 Saxons by himself! What? His little arms must have been aching!

Nennius was writing a couple of hundred years after Arthur died. He probably copied the battle list from an old Welsh battle poem. The trouble is those poems exaggerate just a bit to make their heroes sound like Superman. The truth is (probably) that he was from a Roman family, and led the Brits so well that the Saxons were held back in the south and east of England for forty years.

What story books and history books don't tell you is that the King Arthur from the oldest legends wasn't a goody-goody leader fighting against evil. Arthur could be pretty awful!

Awful Arthur

How about hearing some of the stories about the awful side of Arthur ... ?

Once upon a time, in the middle of Wales, there was a tyrant who came from foreign parts and his name was Arthur. When this Arthur came to the monastery at Llanbadarn Fawr he met the bishop Paternus and he cast his eyes greedily on the bishop's fine tunic. 'Bishop!' said Arthur. 'That is a wonderful tunic and I want it for my own!'

And the bishop replied, 'This tunic is for priests! A wicked man may not wear it, and you are a wicked man.'

Then Arthur fell into a mighty rage and left the monastery, raving furiously. Later that day he returned and found bishop Paternus praying.

Arthur snatched at the bishop's tunic and tried to tear it off him. Arthur cursed and Arthur swore in the sight of God. Arthur stamped on the ground like a child.

Then bishop Paternus said, 'Let the earth swallow him up!'

The earth at once opened in a great crack and swallowed Arthur up to the chin. The wicked king was afraid and begged, 'Forgive me please, Paternus. Forgive me!'

Bishop Paternus, the saint, forgave the greedy king and at once the crack in the earth spewed King Arthur up.

And Arthur was *not* a friend to ladies in distress ...

One day cruel King Arthur was riding with three of his knights when he saw a woman carried on a horse by a man. A troop of soldiers were chasing them.

'Look, Arthur! That lady is being chased by those soldiers! We should help her to escape!' the knights cried.

But when wicked Arthur saw the woman his heart was filled with desire and he wanted her for himself. 'No, my knights!' he cried. 'Take the woman and bring her to me! She's just the sort of lady that I could take for my love!'

'You can't do that!' his knights said.

'I can! I'm king!' the angry Arthur argued.

'We have to help the lady!' the knights said angrily.

Arthur scowled and Arthur fretted and then he said, 'Oh, very well. If you would rather help a lady than grab the girl for me, then go ahead.'

And so the knights rode down and saved the lady and they gave her their protection.

But Arthur, he was not a happy king.

Then there's the idea that Arthur was a 'religious' king who fought under the Christian cross against the pagan Saxons.

At the battle of Badon Arthur carried the cross of our Lord Jesus Christ on his shoulders for three days and nights and the Britons won victory.

This is the battle where he slew 960 Saxons single handed ... with a cross on his back! Did he use the cross to batter the 960 to death? Whew! What a man!

But hang on ... another old story says he took the altar from a church and used it to eat his dinner! Would a good Christian do that? So much for a knight of the round table – he was more like a knight of the nicked table.

And what would the noble Arthur do to a brave enemy? Spare his life and make him a friend? No chance ...

In farthest Scotland was a warrior prince and this man's name was Cuill. Now Cuill was a brave warrior and a famous soldier who bowed down to no king, not even Arthur.

He would often come down from Scotland, burning and raiding and winning great victories. And Arthur, the king of all Britain, heard what this gallant young man was doing. Many people hoped Cuill would take Arthur's place one day, but Arthur sought him out and murdered him.

After the murder Arthur went home, feeling very happy to have killed such a strong enemy.

So there you have another view of Arthur. Thief and murderer with no respect for women or the Church. These story writers were writing long after Arthur's death, but it's interesting that, at the time, no one argued with the way they described him – as a wicked man. Take your pick:

THE GREAT ARTHUR DEBATE

| BRAVE RESPECTED HERO | GREEDY CRUEL VILLAIN | NOBLE GOD-FEARING KNIGHT | STORY-BOOK LEGEND |
| BRITISH MONK AD 540 | WELSH POET AD 1000 | NORMAN MONK AD 1300 | HISTORIAN AD 2000 |

We'll probably never know the whole truth now. Arthur can be whatever you want him to be.

Naughty nuns and mischievous monks

If you were a Christian Saxon peasant you could escape from the pain of the plough and the foulness of the farm by joining a monastery. The monasteries encouraged parents to send their sons at the age of seven. But it would cost them …

Making monks

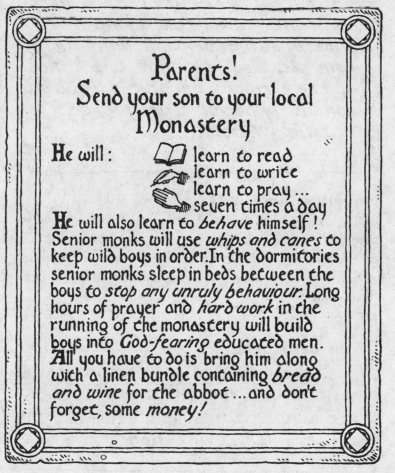

Parents!
Send your son to your local Monastery

He will:
- learn to read
- learn to write
- learn to pray … seven times a day

He will also learn to *behave* himself! Senior monks will use *whips and canes* to keep wild boys in order. In the dormitories senior monks sleep in beds between the boys to *stop any unruly behaviour.* Long hours of prayer and *hard work* in the running of the monastery will build boys into *God-fearing* educated men. All you have to do is bring him along with a linen bundle containing *bread* and *wine* for the abbot … and don't forget, some *money!*

What they didn't mention was that life could be hard. The Abbot of Monkwearmouth, a monastery in north-eastern England, wrote a letter to a friend in Germany and said:

> During the past winter our island has been savagely troubled with cold and ice and with long and widespread storms of wind and rain. It is so bad that the hands of the writers become numb and cannot produce a very large number of books.

Naughty nuns

You worked and prayed and prayed and worked. You were supposed to lead a simple, holy life, but many monks and nuns enjoyed life a bit more than they were supposed to.

Some Saxon letters have survived with complaints a bit like this one ...

> My dear abbess,
>   I was shocked and horrified on my visit to your convent. I expected to see holy women, simply and modestly dressed. What did I find?

> × Nuns who crimped their hair with curling irons.
> × Nuns wearing brightly coloured head-dresses laced with ribbons down to their ankles.
> × Nuns with sharpened fingernails like hawks' talons.
>
> I hope these disgraceful practices will cease immediately.
>
> Angry from Tunbridge Wells

And many monks were no better. The monk-historian Bede told the story of Coldingham monastery in Northumbria:

> The cells that were built for praying were turned into places of feasting and drinking.

A Celt called Adamnan warned that he had a dream in which he saw the monastery destroyed. The Coldingham monks behaved themselves for a while after Adamnan's warning.

Then they went back to their old ways and the monastery was destroyed by fire in AD 679. Bede said the fire was God's punishment.

So, be warned!

In 734 Bede himself was complaining in a letter to the Bishop of York:

Your Grace,

As you are aware, a monk vows to lead a single life, without the company of women. I was disgusted to note that monks in one of your monasteries were not only married – they were living in the monastery with their wives and children!

Bede also whinged about priests. They were guilty of 'laughter, jokes, stories, feasting and drunkenness'. Bede would not be someone you'd want to invite to your school Christmas party, then.

Even a strict monastery like Bede's own Monkwearmouth had problems with boys who preferred playing to praying. Just fifty years after Bede's death a monk was complaining that boys at Monkwearmouth monastery were having a wild time hunting foxes and hares! Monk Alcuin wrote:

How wicked to leave the service of Christ for a fox hunt

Misery for monks

Some monasteries could be very strict in their discipline. Boys were beaten with canes or whips for any misbehaviour. (Like dripping hot candle-wax on to an old monk's bald patch!)

But growing up didn't save you! Any monk could be punished by:

- beatings
- being locked in a cell alone
- being fed only bread and water.

Monks who did something really wicked (like eating meat on a Friday) would be thrown out of the monastery.

Just like schools until the 1960s really.

Nasty for nuns

Women had their own monasteries, called convents, but often shared mixed monasteries with monks. It's no surprise that the nuns got all the cooking and cleaning, sewing and serving jobs, is it?

Girls who became nuns must have liked larking about the way girls do today because there were rules to stop them. So, in the bedrooms, the nuns slept in rows – and the young nuns had old nuns sleeping between them to stop any joking, bullying or pillow fights (as girls tend to do, so they tell me).

But the naughtiest nun crime was 'vanity' – admiring your own good looks and sitting around in front of mirrors all day.

The nuns brought in one strict rule:

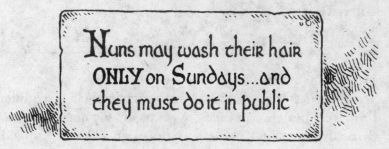

Nuns may wash their hair ONLY on Sundays...and they must do it in public

How would you like *that* rule, girls?

Suffering saints

Monks spent much of their time writing out the lives of saints. The tales of these weird and wonderful men and women were as exciting as a *Horrible Histories* book – but as believable as Enid Blyton!

Still, a saint's day was a good excuse for a holiday, so here are some excuses for a few days off from school. Just tell teacher you're a Saxon! You make up your own mind as to how true some of the curious cases on the calendar are.

24 Feb

Saint Ethelbert
Born: late 500s
Died: 616

In 597 all England was a pagan country. Then Saint Augustine landed in King Ethelbert's kingdom and Eth said, 'I shall not harm you,' which was pretty nice, for a Saxon. King Eth not only made St Gus welcome but had himself and most of his people converted to Christianity.

This was the first ever Christian kingdom in England, so Eth became a saint. He didn't have to starve or suffer some other horrible death! Even you could be a saint if it's that easy!

Celebrate by going up to a passing monk and saying, 'I will not harm you!'

19 May

Saint Dunstan
Born: 909
Died: 988

A top saint in late Saxon Britain. Started in the court of King Athelstan – but Dun was given the boot for being a magician (no, not the sort that waves wands and pulls rabbits out of hats). Yet Dun *did* seem to have magic powers because he saw the murder of King Edmund before it happened (but never got to warn dead Ed). And an angel appeared on the road to tell Dun that King Eadred was dying – the shock of meeting the angel actually killed Dun's horse!

Dun set up a monastery and a school and for that he became a saint. Would you make your school teacher a saint?

Celebrate by waving a magic wand and making your school disappear!

23 June

Saint Etheldreda
Born: early 600s
Died: late 600s

A Saxon princess who wanted to become a nun but had to get married. Happily her husband died ... well, not so happily for him. But, would you believe it, she had to take a second husband. She was such a miserable wife he eventually divorced her and let her get on with her nunning. She gave up fine clothes and wore rough wool, only washed with cold water and caught the plague. Like most plague victims she had a dirty great lump on her neck. She said, 'This is God's punishment because I once wore a rich necklace there! Cccct!' and she died. When her coffin was opened 16 years after her death the lump on her neck was ... gone! She became the saint of people with sore throats.

Celebrate by washing your wool shirt in cold water, throwing away your necklaces and marrying twice.

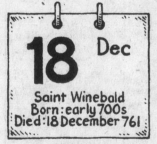

18 Dec

Saint Winebald
Born: early 700s
Died: 18 December 761

Saxon Winebald went off to Rome with his dad and his brother Willibald. (Note: I did not make up these silly names. Blame their dad, Saint Richard the Saxon.) Anyway, he set up a monastery in Germany and built a nunnery next door for his sister Walburga to run. Winebald was a poorly old man but he battled on bravely through great pain to do this Christian work. At least he got to be a saint when he died.

Celebrate by taking an aspirin – and writing a letter to your parents: 'Dear parents, thanks for not calling me Walburga, Winebald or Willibald!'

Saxon skills

Saxons had to have lots of skills to make the things they needed. Take something simple like making leather. Would you have the stomach for this lousy job?

Lousy leather

Animal skin rots and lets in water unless it is 'tanned' to turn it into leather. That's something even cave people knew and they made the animal skins into leather by pounding them with animal fat and brains! If they turned the leather into wooden-soled shoes they'd have real clever clogs! (Oh, never mind.)

Anyway, Lloyds Bank in York is on the site of a Saxon leather-making shop – a 'tannery'. Archaeologists dug there and found some interesting – but disgusting – facts about Saxon leather ...

You can imagine a Saxon warrior running away from a battle with the Vikings and claiming it was his shoes that ran away ... 'cos they were chicken!

Monk-y business

Making books was even messier than making leather. Monks used to murder kids to make books! Nah! I mean young goats – kids. What did you think I meant? They also massacred lambs and cut up calves in their thousands.

When well-behaved monks weren't praying, working in the fields, praying, helping the poor and needy, praying, sleeping in an unheated room, praying, eating some foul mush ... or praying ... they wrote books. Because printing hadn't been invented, they mostly copied other books by hand – the Bible and lives of saints and other people's work. Some brilliant monks, like Bede, wrote new books, including the first history of the English people.

There was also a whole horrible industry of monks providing the writing materials, because a monk couldn't pop down to the local corner shop for a pencil and paper. They hadn't been invented either! No, a lot of lambs and calves had to die to make those books.

NOTE: Vegetarians should skip this section.

Monks wrote on sheets of animal skin called 'vellum'. This is how you make vellum.

TRIM THE EDGES STRAIGHT AND KEEP THEM BETWEEN WOODEN BOARDS SO THEY DON'T CURL BACK UP INTO THE CUTE LITTLE SHAPE OF A CUTE LITTLE LAMB'S BELLY

The books from the 500s were all made on good quality skins. But by the end of the Dark Ages there were so many monks murdering so many lambs and calves and goats that they became a bit careless about the scraping and the vellum is sometimes as rough as a badger's bum.

Perfect pens and ideal ink
Next you needed a pen made from a stiff bird's feather, or quill. This was not quite as cruel as making the vellum because you didn't have to kill the birds to take their quills!

Take a seagull's or a goose's feather – it won't hurt much. (It's no more cruel than sneaking up behind a teacher and pulling a clump of their hair out with one sharp tug.) Wash the feather in hot water, then dry it. Trim off the feathery part with a sharp knife (careful!) to leave only the central shaft. Now you need to cut the end square. Finally cut away the back of the nib and make a slit half a centimetre up the shaft.

So now we've got the paper, or vellum, and pen. Of course being a big-brained *Horrible Histories* reader you'll have spotted what's missing. That's right … ink!

Who has to suffer to make the ink? Intsy-winsy baby wasps, that's who …

Did you know … ?

One book that remains from the early 700s is called *The Lindisfarne Gospels*. It took the skin of at least 129 calves so it's not suitable for reading by vegetarians.

You are only able to read this *Horrible Histories* book because monks wrote down all that history. Thousands of creatures died so you could read this book!

I hope you feel ashamed of yourself!

Games you wouldn't want to play

Life could be cruel and so sports could be crueler. Don't try these at home …

Pony clubbing
What you need:
Two stallion horses
(bad tempered ones are best)
A square of fencing
A couple of sharp sticks

How to play:

Put the two stallions in the square together. They will start to fight. (If they're in a good mood then jab them with sticks to make them wild.)

I THINK THIS ONE'S WILD NOW

Urge the stallions to attack each other with teeth and hooves. The winner is the first stallion to flatten the other.

How to win:

Bet on the horse you think will win.

Bull-baiting

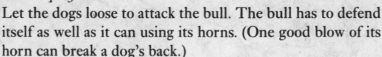

What you need:

A bull chained to a wooden stake
Dogs

How to play:

Let the dogs loose to attack the bull. The bull has to defend itself as well as it can using its horns. (One good blow of its horn can break a dog's back.)

How to win:

Bet on how many dogs the bull can kill.

Did you know … ?

Christian Saxons were expected to give up drinking in the weeks leading up to Easter. The writer Aelfric told of a man who broke this rule. He got very drunk, wandered out into the street where a bull was being baited and was gored to death by the bull. Aelfric said this was God's punishment on the drinker. But then God didn't punish the bull-baiters!

Terrible truths or foul fibs?

Truth is stranger than fiction, someone very clever and very boring once said. But you have to be able to tell the difference.

First take a passing parent (or priest) and sit them in a chair. (You may have to tie them there, so have a clothes-line handy.)

Say: 'You have to help me with my homework!' Then pester your parent (or perplex your priest) with this cunning cwiz and see if they can sort out the truth from the fibs.

1 The Saxons played bagpipes.

2 The Saxons dressed in nettles.

3 The Saxons built their houses out of pig poo.

4 Saxon shepherds were paid with cattle dung.

5 Saxon gold coins were often fakes because they didn't have a test for gold.

6 The Vikings raided Saxon towns when they knew they would be deserted.

7 The wheelbarrow was invented in Saxon times.

8 If someone wanted half a penny in Saxon times then they cut a penny coin in half.

Answers:

1 True … probably! They certainly had flutes and trumpets, harps and whistles, but some archaeologists believe they had bagpipes too.

OH HOW I WISH THE ARCHAEOLOGISTS WERE WRONG

2 True. The stems of the nettles were crushed and dried. They could then be woven into a cloth to make clothes. Imagine wearing nettle knickers!

3 True. First they planted posts in the ground, then wove branches between the posts. But there were lots of gaps. The walls had to be plastered with mud, though pig droppings could be slapped on and would dry to make a nice hard wall. Don't you wonder how they trained the pigs to poo on the walls? Hey! You don't suppose the Saxons just went around picking the stuff up in their bare hands, do you?

4 True. The shepherd was given 12 days' supply of cattle droppings as a special Christmas treat. He could spread it over his fields as fertilizer. Shepherds were also allowed to keep one lamb and one fleece each year in payment. Maybe you'd like to revive this old Saxon custom and give a few buckets of manure to your best friend on Christmas Day? Then again, you may prefer to give it to your worst enemy.

5 False. The Saxons weren't great scientists but they did know how to test for gold. The king had a water butt with a fixed level of water in it. He took a certain weight of metal. If it was gold the water rose to just below the brim. If some cheap metal had been mixed in then the water overflowed. Water clever lot they were!

6 False. The Vikings raided on holy days when they knew the towns would be full of pilgrims, women and children going to church. These unarmed people would be snatched and sold as slaves as far away as north Africa. The Saxons weren't a lot better – the church objected to *Christians* like themselves being sold as slaves; they didn't object to other people being made slaves.

7 True. BUT ... not by the Saxons. It was invented by the Chinese and won't be seen in Europe till the 1200s. The Saxons hadn't even invented buttons – they had to use brooches and cords.

8 True. Don't try cutting a pound coin in half if your local sweet shop wants 50p – it's now against the law.

Awful Offa, Alf and Ath

An Offa lot of wealth

In 757 King Aethelbald (who wasn't bald), king of the Mercians, died. He was a tough old goat who chased women – and often caught them! He was also very violent. Of course some people didn't like him and he got himself murdered by the men who were supposed to protect him – his bodyguards.

But where did they get the idea to murder their boss? The finger of suspicion points at King Offa who took the throne. Offa went on to rule Mercia in the middle of England – he was the meat in a sandwich of the Northumbrians (the Saxons in the north) and the Saxons of the south. He also had a lot of trouble with the wild Welsh. That's probably why he built a wide ditch and mound to keep them out of his kingdom.

CROSS-SECTION OF OFFA'S DYKE

CROSS-SECTION OF WELSHMAN

Offa also had trouble with the kings in the tribes he took over. They weren't all happy about paying 'tribute' to Offa. Every year they had to meet him and give him payment.

This could be …

- Money, gold brooches and precious metals.
- Cattle and horses, hawks and hounds (for hunting).
- Decorated swords with magical spells on them.
- A feather bed and fine linen bed sheets.

They also had to send men to fight for Offa and almost certainly had to send the men who dug his 150 mile ditch on the Welsh border.

In return Offa's army protected them – or at least didn't destroy them!

Offa his food
Offa also demanded 'food-rent'. He travelled around his kingdom and expected his nobles to feast and entertain him with lots of grub. How would you like the bill for feeding 150 people a day? Bet you hope and pray he doesn't stay a week!

Warning people Offa

One king who grew tired of paying Offa was Aethelberht of
East Anglia. Old coins give us a clue to what happened …

The murder of Aethelberht shocked many Mercians and their other Saxon neighbours – but it kept them in line.

Mercian misery

Offa died in 796 and his son died a few months later. The kings in East Anglia and Kent revolted against the miserable Mercian rule straight away – this was the chance they'd been waiting for.

The rebels of Kent were led by a monk-king Eadberht. He was captured but the merciful Mercians *didn't* execute him, the way Offa would have done.

YEAH! WE JUST CHOPPED HIS HANDS OFF AND GOUGED HIS EYES OUT

THANKS, GUYS!

But the days of Mercian mastery were numbered once their great king hopped Offa the twig. Offa had created the idea that England could be one kingdom with one king. Yet it *wasn't* the Mercians who went on to rule that kingdom – it was the West Saxons.

When Offa died in 796 there were four great Saxon kingdoms in England – his Mercia, Wessex (West Saxons), East Anglia and Northumbria. By 878 only the kingdom of Wessex had survived.

Tough luck Offa, after you went to all that boffa …

What went wrong? The Vikings, that's what.

Silver and geld

The Saxons had come as raiders. Once they'd conquered the Brits they settled down as farmers and forgot how to fight.

So along came the Vikings from Denmark as raiders; they conquered the Saxons and settled down as farmers. If the Saxons could hang on long enough the Vikings might just forget how to fight too!

King Alfred was the first to fight back. But he wasn't quite ready to go into battle. So, at first, he just paid the

Vikings to leave him alone. This payment to the Danish Vikings has become known as 'Danegeld'.

As you'll read later, Ethelred the Unready has been called nasty names by historians because he paid fortunes in Saxon money to the Vikings so they'd go away. But those historians like to forget it was Alfred the 'Great' who did it first!

As a modern poet, Rudyard Kipling wrote, paying Danegeld was a pointless waste of money ...

> *And that is called paying the Dane-geld;*
> *But we've proved it again and again,*
> *That if once you have paid him the Dane-geld*
> *You never get rid of the Dane.*

Did you know ... ?
Saxon coins were made by 'moneyers' in the king's mint. They had the pattern on a stamp and hit the blank discs of silver with the stamp. The seventy mints made as many as five million coins a year this way!

A moneyer could become rich by making each coin just a little bit smaller than he was supposed to and saving all the little scraps of silver to build up a million-scrap fortune. BUT ... Athelred's Code of Laws said ...

> *If a moneyer is found guilty of making coins too small then the hand that committed the crime shall be cut off and fastened to the mint.*

Would that make a good punishment for shop assistants who give short change today?

Alf and Ath fight back

When the Danegeld ran out the Vikings squidged the Wessex king, Alfred, and his few hundred followers on to the marshes at Athelney. Alf broke out and gave the Vikings such a battering they made peace – and their king even became a Christian. Alf christened the Viking leader (Guthrum) himself.

Alf has become an English hero because the history books said he was a great leader. Who had the history books written? Alf, of course.

Alf's grandson, Athelstan, took the throne twenty-five years after Alf died and he set about snatching back all of England from the Viking settlers. He conquered England from Northumbria down to the south coast. Then he set about making the wild Welsh obey him. What a great guy. But Athelstan is forgotten in history books. Why? Because he didn't have history books written about his great victories.

History can be very unfair. It can also be full of fibs.

Hot hero

Alf, for example, is famous for the story of burning the cakes. Alf was in disguise, hiding from the Vikings (they said) when he went to a poor cottage for shelter. As the monks of St Neotts wrote over 250 years after Alf the Great died ...

THE FOLLOWING STORY IS 110% TRUE AND NOT ONE WORD OF A LIE. CROSS MY HEART AND HOPE TO DIE! HONEST! TRUTHFULLY, SINCERELY. THIS IS A LIE-FREE ZONE!

One day a peasant woman, the wife of a cowherd, was making loaves. King Alfred was sitting by the fire, looking after his bow and arrows and other weapons.

The poor woman saw that the loaves she'd put over the fire were burning. She ran up and took them off and scolded the unbeatable king. 'Look there, man! Couldn't you see the loaves were burning? Why didn't you turn them over? I'm sure you'd be the first to eat them if they were nicely done!'

The miserable woman did not realize that this was King Alfred, who had fought so many wars against the pagans and won so many victories.

The story is almost certainly a lie. But it makes Alf look like a struggling soldier, driven to hiding in the hut of a poor woman and getting nagged. What a hero he must have been to rise from that to defeat the Vikings, you'd say. Alfred is remembered for lies like this.

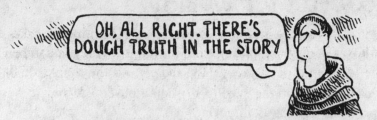

OH, ALL RIGHT. THERE'S DOUGH TRUTH IN THE STORY

Athelstan didn't have historians to lie for him so he's forgotten.

THAT'S HIS FAULT! HE SHOULD HAVE USED HIS LOAF!

But enough of these half-baked jokes.

Woeful for women

Digging up Saxon graves gives us clues about the different jobs men and women did. For example, women's graves often contained sewing boxes, so they must have been responsible for the sewing in their household, and it was probably seen as an important job.

In Saxon poetry women had a hard life and suffered it without complaining. In the real world it probably wasn't all bad. For example, unlike in many periods in history, women could be landowners ... though the only land some women got was a six foot grave.

A grave problem

One early Saxon grave was uncovered in layers. Could *you* be an archaeologist and explain what was most likely to have happened?

Explanation: The rich woman died, was put in her coffin and buried. The coffin was covered with a layer of soil and the second woman was thrown in – alive. The stone was placed on top of her to keep her there while the soil was piled on top to bury her alive.

It's harder to explain 'Why?' The second woman was possibly a slave sent to serve the rich woman in the afterlife. As if it wasn't bad enough being a slave in *this* life!

The key to success

In some women's graves there are sets of keys. This was a sign that women looked after the family's possessions and ran the house. (It makes you wonder how they got back in the house after the funeral when the keys were six foot under!)

Saxon law said that if stolen money was found in her house, the woman of the house was not to blame – unless it was found in a place she had the keys to.

And if a stolen animal was found in her house then the woman would not be blamed, so long as she swore not to eat the meat!

Wife weplacement

Divorce was rare ... but there was another way to take a second wife while the first one was still alive. If your wife was carried away by an enemy you must try to buy her back. But, if you can't afford to pay for her then you can take a new wife instead!

If a man was fed up with his first wife (and that has been known to happen) then he must have been tempted to go around making enemies. But there must have been a bit of girl-power in Saxon times. If a man was captured by an enemy then a wife could take a new husband the same way.

YOO-HOO! MR VI-KING! MY HUSBAND'S OVER THERE!

Mystic mugs

Crystal balls have been found in some Saxon graves – usually the graves of women. These wise women used them to tell the future and were called 'heahrune'.

But if a wise woman used her mystic powers to work wicked magic then she was called a 'haegtessan' ... a witch. And some still use the word 'hag' to insult a woman. (But *you* would never, ever, ever use such words about your teacher, would you?)

The witches

If you were a Saxon you probably believed that demons in the dark had the power to make a deal with you! They would give you magical powers on Earth ... but as soon as you died then the Devil himself would come and take you away. If you agreed to that deal then you became a witch.

There is a story of a Saxon woman in the 800s who made such a deal with the Devil. Her story was turned into a poem a thousand years later by the Poet Laureate, Robert Southey (1774–1843)[1]. When the Devil sent his messenger raven, the old woman knew her time was up ...

The Devil's Due

The raven croaked as she sat at her meal,
And the old woman knew what he said.
And she grew pale at the raven's tale,
And sickened and went to bed.

'I've anointed myself with infant's fat.
The devils have been my slaves.
From sleeping babes I have sucked the breath,
I have called the dead from their graves.

'And the Devil will fetch me now in fire,
My witchcraft to atone;
And I, who have troubled the dead man's grave
Shall have no rest in my own.'

1. The 'Poet Laureate' is supposed to be Britain's best living poet of the time. He (it's always been a 'he') is paid by the king or queen to write royal poems from time to time. Sadly being made 'Poet Laureate' doesn't mean you're always a very good poet.

They blest the old woman's winding sheet
With rites and prayers that were due.
With holy water they sprinkled her shroud,
And they sprinkled her coffin too.

And in he came with eyes of flame –
The Devil to fetch the dead.
And all the church in his presence glowed
Like a fiery furnace red.

He laid his hands on the iron chains;
And like flax they mouldered asunder.
And the coffin lid which was barred so firm
He burst with his voice of thunder.

And he called the old woman of Berkeley to rise
And come with her master away.
A cold sweat started on that cold corpse,
And the voice she was forced to obey.

The devil he flung her on a horse,
And he leapt up before.
And away like the lightning's speed she went;
And she was seen no more.

You'll notice the 'witch' was an old woman. The Saxons believed the Devil could possess a man *or* a woman, but there were many old tales such as this where women were the main suspects. Old women could not defend themselves so it was easy to accuse them of witchcraft and punish them.

Being a Saxon woman had its problems.

Did you know … ?

A Saxon man could suffer an 'illness' from 'a woman's chatter'! It had its own cure like many other illnesses.

Men's Own Saxon Weekly

CUT THE CACKLE

Have you ever had a hard day on the farm only to come home to an earful of woman's talk? Are you needlessly nagged? Does gossip make you gag? In short, do you suffer from a woman's chatter?

Then old Doctor Bald's leechbook has the answer!

Just take a radish – yes one of those hot, red veggies – and eat it before you go to bed. But beware, boys – eat nothing else!

Next morning the woman may still be wittering but you'll find it no longer bothers you!

Of course men today just love listening to women talk!

The cruel cave

The trouble with being a woman in Saxon times was that the world was run by men. Your life was decided by your father while you were a child, and your husband when you were married. That may have been fine for many women. But if a husband had problems then his wife would suffer too … maybe even worse!

There is an old Saxon poem called 'The Wife's Lament' preserved in *The Exeter Book* that's kept now in Exeter Cathedral. It's about a woman who came from overseas to marry a man. The man didn't tell her that he was mixed up in a feud and he soon had to escape to save his life. She was left behind, in a strange land, and had to live hidden in a cave beneath an oak tree.

The Saxon poets would go to feasts and sing her sad story ...

I've never known such misery since I became his wife,
Abandoned by a husband who sailed off to save his life.

A victim of a vicious feud, he had to leave me here,
And hide me deep within these woods where I must live in fear.

I live beneath an ancient oak, within a deep earth cave,
Alive, and yet it seems to me, I'm living in my grave.

Each dawn I rise and leave the cave to walk through twisted trees,
And moan when I remember how my lord is overseas.

Sad grief is all there is for those who have to live apart.
No friends, no parents and no love. Alone with aching heart.

It's enough to put you off your feast, isn't it?

I suppose it's no worse than watching some miserable television programme while you're chewing your chips or slurping your soup.

We'll have none of that ear

A married woman in late Saxon times could *not* go off with another man. If she did, the church law said …

> …*her husband shall take all her property and she is to lose her nose and ears.*

Married men didn't suffer that punishment if they went off with another woman. This law didn't last long and was changed in 1035.

What would the world be like if we had that law today? Who nose?

Saxon scoffers

No baked beans, no chocolate, no chips. Would you really like to have lived in those days? Like most other ages in horrible history a lot might depend on whether you were a rich noble or a pathetic peasant. For example …

Gut grub
Take 10 jars of honey, 300 loaves of bread, 42 casks of ale, 2 oxen, 10 geese, 20 hens, 10 cheeses, 1 barrel of butter, 5 salmon and 100 eels. What have you got?
1 The food supply for one peasant family for one year?
2 The food supply for one rich farmer for one year?
3 The food eaten by a Saxon king and his friends in one *night*?
The last one, of course. There's no mention of how many indigestion tablets they needed next day.

Putrid pottage
Peasant food was plain and boring. The bread was coarse with grit from the grinding stones. Saxon skeletons found by archaeologists have teeth worn away by chewing bread like sandpaper.

Monasteries grew their own food but it could be pretty boring stuff. A vegetable stew (called 'pottage') would have been a common meal. If you'd like to know how the monks ate then try this recipe ...

Monks' Mush (or Nuns' Nosh)

Here's a tasty treat for you starving sisters and brothers. Eat this three times a day to grow healthy and fit. You may not live to thirty with a potty pottage diet – but life will be so miserable you'll be happy to die!

You need:
1 leek
1 onion
half cup of peas
half cup of lentils
half litre of water
pinch of parsley
pinch of sage
salt

Cooking:
Peel and chop the onion and the leek.
Boil the water and add the parsley, sage and salt.
Add the onion, leek, peas and lentils.
Cover and boil slowly for half an hour.
Serve with thick chunks of bread.

You may enjoy this recipe. But if you try eating it three times a day, seven days a week for most of your life, you may just get a teeny-weeny bit bored with it.

Run, rabbit, run!

St Benedict made the rules that monks lived by. One rule said they should not eat flesh. But monks took this to mean they should not eat four-legged animals. They ate fish and birds – and they even ate beavers because (they said) beavers live in water, so they're fish! But, strangest of all, the Normans brought rabbits to Britain when they conquered it in 1066, and monks decided it was all right to eat them!

Test your teacher on taste

Ask your teacher these questions about Saxon food. See if they can score ten out of ten! Which of these foods did Saxons eat?

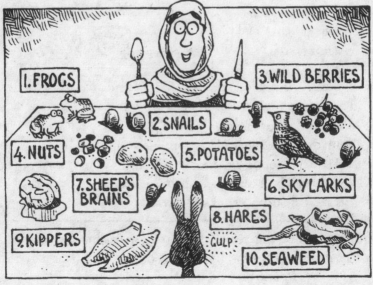

78

Hunger horrors

Some of the things Saxons ate may seem disgusting to you – you don't see many sheep brains on the school dinner menu, do you? But there was something worse than eating seaweed sandwiches, and that was eating nothing at all.

Food didn't keep for very long – no fridges in Saxon houses. You grew food in summer and ate it over the winter. But if you failed to grow the food in the summer then you starved over winter.

What would stop you growing food in summer? Well ...

- Bad weather, heavy rain, floods or storms destroying your wheat.
- Viking invaders burning your fields and stealing your cattle.
- Plagues killing off farm workers and animal plagues destroying your flocks.

What could you do?

- Jump off a cliff.
- Eat your neighbours.
- Sell your children.
- Put your head in your lord's hands.
- Eat a tree.

Do they sound daft? Well they're horribly historically true, as the chronicles of the time tell ...

OUR FAMINE FAVOURITES

Crops failed? Got a rumbling tum? Then try these top tips from the *Anglo-Saxon Chronicle* and see how you can cure those hunger pains!

1 Fall in line

In Sussex last year forty villagers cured their hunger for good. They went to the edge of a cliff, joined hands and jumped over. The ones who weren't crushed on the rocks were drowned in the sea. Fast food for fish!

2 Funeral food

It's been reported that when villagers died in a famine area they were not buried by their families (as that would be a waste of good meat). Instead they were cooked and eaten. Human hotpot saves lives.

3 Slave away

The Saxon law says: 'A father may sell a son if that child is under seven years old and if he needs to do so.' Selling children earns you money … plus you save because you don't have to feed them! No kids is good kids – no kidding!

4 Good Lord!

It is a lord of the manor's duty to protect his people. If the worst comes to the worst visit your local lord, kneel in front of him and place your head in his hands. You then become his slave and work for him – but at least he'll feed you.

5 Tree-mendous!

When all else fails you can eat everything in sight. It's been reported that Saxon survivors ground up anything from acorns to tree-bark, nettles and wild grass to fill out the flour. Your bark can be good for your bite!

Muttering monks

It's nice to sit down at a table, eat good food and gossip with a friend. But monks were supposed to be silent while they ate their food. That's not just boring ... it can also be a real nuisance. What about if you need something desperately? Don't worry – the monks had their own system of signs.

Try eating school dinners in silence (your teachers will like this historical game!) and use the monk system instead of words. Here are four to get you started.

Monastery messages

1. 'Pass the salt' – place three fingers together and shake them as if salting something

2. 'Pass the pepper' – knock two fingers together

3. 'Pour me some wine' – put thumb and forefinger together as if turning on the tap of a cask

4. 'Pass the butter' – stroke three fingers of one hand over the palm of the other hand

There are an amazing 127 different signs in the monks' guidebook that you'd have to learn. Once you've mastered the four above then make up your own ... but I don't want to see the one you make up for 'I think I'll go for a pee'.

Horrible historical joke
This witty riddle was written by a monk ...

QUESTION: WHAT MAKES BITTER THINGS SWEET?
ANSWER: HUNGER

It's not a very good joke, but it's survived 1200 years, which is more than you will, so don't sneer at it!

Did you know ... ?
November was known as 'Blood Month'. That month was when the Saxons slaughtered cattle because (a) they wanted to eat them over the winter months, and (b) they couldn't feed many of the beasts when there was no fresh grass. So it was bye-bye to your old friend Daisy the cow and hello to scrumptious steaks. Could you eat your old friend?

Sooty bacon
Saxon houses had no chimneys – the smoke just drifted upwards and out through a hole in the roof. When a pig was killed for food it was hung from the roof and the smoke 'cured' it; that is, it stopped it going bad. So a pig killed in autumn could still be eaten in spring.

And people today still enjoy the taste of smoked bacon. But modern smoky bacon is probably not as tasty as Saxon bacon which would have bits of soot from below, not to mention insects dropping down from the roof. Nothing nicer than a sprinkling of spider to add to your breakfast bacon!

The Tudors brought tobacco to Britain so maybe they invented the horrible historical joke ...

Bee brave and bee have!

There was no sugar in Saxon England. The only sweetener was honey, so a family celebrated when bees set up a hive in their roof.

There was one sure way of persuading bees to come to your home. When a swarm flies past you, grab a handful of gravel and throw it over them, crying the spell:

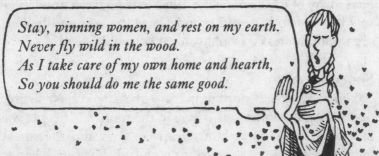

Stay, winning women, and rest on my earth.
Never fly wild in the wood.
As I take care of my own home and hearth,
So you should do me the same good.

Of course it may be dangerous to throw gravel at a swarm of bees. So get the nearest teacher to do it for you while you go inside and shut the doors and windows.

Curious cures

Luckily some marvellous medicine books have survived from the Saxon age. Books like *Bald's Leechbook* (Bald was the owner of the book) written in the late 800s. Some of the magical charms go back to Saxon days before they invaded England and are probably the oldest pieces of German writing we have.

Curl curing

The Saxons had their own treatments for baldness. You can't buy it at Boots, but you may like to offer a bald bloke you know this cure ...

**HORRIBLE HISTORIES®
HAIR RESTORER**

Is your Dad (or your history teacher) a slaphead? Is there more hair on a hen's egg than his skull's skin?

Then try Horrible Histories hair restorer!

Yes, this is simply made by burning bees and rubbing the ash into the shining scalp.

This wonder cure is absolutely free – and you get your money back if it doesn't work! You'll be your parent's pet for ever more!

Helping your hair gives me a real buzz!

You're a honey!

Or you could buy a wig.

Cute cures

Pagan and Christian ideas were mixed up when Saxons tried to cure sicknesses. Could you cure these six Saxons' sicknesses? (Cure it! You couldn't even say it!)

1.
For a toothache

2.
For a swelling on the eyelid

3.
For a snake bite

4.
For madness

5.
For a sick horse

6.
For a sick girl

a.
Take the skin of a dolphin, make it into a whip and beat yourself with it

b.
Boil a holly leaf, lay it on a saucer of water, raise to the mouth and yawn

c.
Cut the sign of the cross in the forehead, back and limbs, pierce the left ear, then beat with a stick

  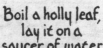 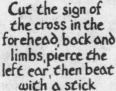

d.
Cut a vein and let out some blood. This must be done at night

e.
Take a knife and cut out the affected part

f.
Take a piece of wood from a tree grown in Heaven and press it to the wound

86

Answers:

1b) You will find (a Saxon medical book promises) that 'the evil tooth-worms will tumble from the mouth'. Yeuch! Think I'd prefer the toothache!

2e) A Saxon book says that a youth survived a knife through the eyelid. Even kings and queens suffered a bit of butchery. Queen Etheldrida had a swelling on her jaw and her doctor 'opened the swelling to let out the poisonous matter in it'. She'd have cried 'Ouch' but it's difficult crying anything with a knife in your jaw!

3f) You might well ask, 'How do you get wood from a tree grown in Heaven?' Well that's a stupid question, if I may say so. Just let the snakebite kill you, go to Heaven and get the wood to cure you. Simple!

SORRY. NOT STOPPING. JUST POPPED UP FOR A BIT OF TIMBER

4a) You may not be mad after the whipping – but the skinless dolphin will be absolutely furious.

5c) This treatment will make your horse a little cross – or six little crosses, to be accurate. You may find that your local vet does not use this old Saxon cure.

6d) A Saxon bishop warned doctors, 'Do not do this on the fourth day of a new moon!' What sort of clock did he use to measure the timing of the moon? A lunar-tick, of course!

Don't try these cures at home because you need the right magical spells to recite with the cure. When the Saxons became Christian the magical spells became Christian prayers – they would sing 'Misere me deus'[1] three times and recite the Lord's Prayer nine times.

Some other cures you probably shouldn't try ...
1 Poisonous spider bite Make three cuts into the flesh near the bite. Let the blood run into a hazel-wood spoon. Throw the spoon *and* blood over the road. Messy!

2 Dog bite Burn the jaw of a pig to ashes. Sprinkle the ashes on to the wound. Mind the pig jaw doesn't bite you too!
3 Bleeding wound To stop the bleeding take the soot from a pot, rub it into a powder and sprinkle it on the wound. If that doesn't work then take fresh horse droppings, bake them dry and rub them into a powder – put the powder on to a thick linen cloth and bind it on to the wound overnight. Yeuch! Better to bleed!
4 Thick hair To thin your hair, burn a swallow to ashes and rub the ashes into the scalp. To completely stop hair growing then rub ant eggs into the scalp. What a yolk!

1. It means 'God have mercy on me'. You can try singing that instead and just hope that God speaks English!

5 Headache Take swallow-chicks and cut them open. Look for little stones in their stomachs, sew them into a bag and place on the head. This is also a cure for people plagued by goblins.

EEK!

OH NO! HE'S GOT SWALLOW-CHICK-STOMACH-STONES ON HIS HEAD!

Cuthbert's cure

If you are ill it helps to be a saint. When St Cuthbert had a swollen knee he was advised to cook wheat flour with milk and put the hot mixture on his knee. Who told him this? His doctor? No. An angel on a horse! (Why did the angel need a horse? Weren't his wings working? And if the angel is God's messenger, then why didn't God just cure the knee without all that gooey flour? Or why did God allow Cuthbert's knee to swell in the first place? Sometimes God can be a funny woman.)

Health horrors

The good news is Saxon adults were quite tall and strong. History lessons often say that people in the past were much smaller and weedier than we are today. That may have been true for the children of Queen Victoria's smoky slums. It wasn't true of the Saxons. (Archaeologists have measured the Saxon bones in graves and proved this. Nice job, eh?)

The bad news is only half the Saxons lived to see their 25th birthday.

More bad news is that there were a lot of diseases that couldn't be cured and were quite nasty.

Four foul health horrors that Saxons lived and died with were ...

1 Fleas Monks had four or five baths every year – outside the monasteries people probably had fewer – so fleas flew happily through clothes, scoffed on your skin and belched after a bellyful of your blood. One wacky cure was to take the flea-infested clothes and lock them in an air-tight box. They must have thought the fleas would starve or suffocate!

2 Lice These stubborn little friends lay their eggs in your hair and cling like a rottweiler to a burglar's bum. The Saxons used combs with very close teeth, dragged them through the hair and hoped to pull out the eggs and the lice – not to mention lumps of hair! St Cuthbert was buried with a comb made from an elephant's tusk – he must have had jumbo-sized lice!

3 Ergot Old grain went mouldy with a fungus called ergot. If you made the grain into flour and ate the fungus you got ergotism ... very nasty. If you are lucky you feel anxious, and dizzy, get noises in your ears, feel your arms and legs are on fire and can't stop them twitching. You dance out of control ... but could recover. If you were unlucky you got the feeling of ants running round in your burning feet and fingers, which then turned red, then black, then dropped off. If you were really unlucky your ears and nose dropped off and you died. (But ergot was worse in France in the Dark Ages than in England, where victims usually recovered.)

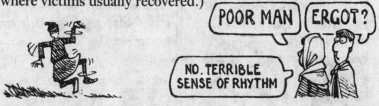

4 Worms No, not the sort of squiggly, fat things you see in the ground. These were the ones that lived inside your body. The whipworm was harmless and stayed in your gut, but the monstrous maw-worm could grow to 30 centimetres and infest your liver or lungs. It could move through your body and pop out anywhere – including the corner of your eye! Yeuch!

Did you know ...?
The Saxons had no idea of how diseases are spread by germs. If food fell on the floor amongst the dog droppings they'd just wipe it (to take away the taste) and make a sign of the cross (to take away any evil spirits that were hanging round there) ... and then pop it into their mouth. Scrummy!

Ethelred the Ready for Beddy

Kwick king kwiz

King Ethelred II was given the name Ethelred 'the Unready'. How have teachers explained this nickname?

HE WAS UNREADY BECAUSE HE WAS NEVER READY WHEN THE VIKINGS INVADED

ETHELRED COULDN'T READ – HE WAS UN-READ, AS THEY SAY

THE SAXON WORD 'RAED' MEANS ADVICE. ETHELRED REFUSED TO TAKE ADVICE, SO HE WAS 'UN-RAEDY'

'RAED' MEANS ADVICE – BUT HE WAS 'UN-RAED' BECAUSE HE WAS GIVEN BAD ADVICE

Answer: At some time or another ALL of these different explanations have been given. The nickname was first written down two hundred years after his death but it could have been used during his lifetime. It was probably meant as a joke – Ethelred was both badly advised (un-raed) AND not ready for the Viking invasions.

And that's not the only unkind thing historians have said about Eth the pathetic...

Unready, steady, go

Poor old Ethelred the Unready came to the throne in 978 and ruled until 1013. He has been remembered for a thousand years as one of the world's worst monarchs – and, as most monarchs have been pretty bad, that means Eth must have been totally useless!

Eth has been blamed for letting the Vikings return and rob the English till their purses and bellies were as empty as a traffic warden's heart. How did Eth get a thousand years of blame?

A hundred years after his death a monk, William of Malmesbury, wrote ...

> *The king was always ready for sleep and it was what he did best. He put off great matters like stopping the Danish Vikings and yawned. If he ever raised the strength to get up on one elbow then he fell back again, either because he couldn't be bothered or because he was driven back by bad luck.*

Of course Will of Malmesbury didn't mean Eth really spent all his time in bed. He just meant he was as dozy as someone who did. Yet Eth spent 38 years on the throne – so he must have been doing something right! And he didn't have a lot going for him:

- Bad-tempered, violent King Edward was murdered so his half-brother Ethelred could become king – church leaders made evil Edward a saint.
- Edward was murdered while he was visiting Ethelred – churchmen said killing the king brought a curse on Eth, even if he wasn't to blame for it.

- Eth was just ten years old when he took the throne – would you rule a country at that age?
- 'A cloud as red as blood' was seen after Eth was crowned – it appeared at midnight and vanished at dawn – it was a sign that God was angry.

Byrhtnoth the brave (but batty)

Eth wasn't the only one to blame for the Viking success. Byrhtnoth was an old but brave Saxon warrior. The Vikings landed on the little island of Northey in the River Blackwater near Maldon, Essex. Byrhtnoth's army faced them from the bank of the river, across the shallow water, and their fate was recorded in the heroic poem, 'The Battle of Maldon'.

First the Vikings demanded payment ...

Bold Byrhtnoth replied ...

Tough talk!

The island was joined to the shore by a strip of mud at low tide. As the Vikings tried to cross Byrhtnoth's men cut them down.

The Vikings said …

Byrhtnoth! We cannot fight like this. Let my men cross to the shore and give you a real battle!

What a joke! A wise old warrior would say, 'No!' In fact only a bird-brained booby would say, 'Yes.'

Byrhtnoth said, 'Yes.'

Byrhtnoth was a brave and heroic man. He was soon a brave and heroic corpse as the Vikings cut him and his men to pieces.

But at least he *tried* to fight back. King Ethelred simply said …

PAY THEM!

Gruesome at Greenwich

Ethelred had a fair idea of what might happen if he didn't pay the Vikings. Look at what happened to Archbishop Aelfheah!

If one of the serving women at a Viking stronghold could have written, this is how she may have described the grisly scene …

Greenwich
Near London
20 April 1012

Dear Mum,

I am sending you a
few pieces of silver. I pinched
them from the Danish Vikings here.
Don't worry, they won't miss them —
and anyway, they owe me the money
after the way they've made me work!
'I'm not a slave!' I told them. At least
I would have told them but I was a
bit scared they'd make me one!

Anyway, last week they started
collecting that tribute Ethelred and
us Saxons have to pay. 48,000
pounds in silver! Agnes, who speaks
a bit of Viking, says they were
boasting that it would be about
twelve million silver coins!

But last night they turned really

nasty. They robbed a trade ship on the river Thames and pinched barrels and barrels of French wine. Of course, being Vikings, they had to drink it all in one feast, didn't they? I was run off my feet keeping their goblets topped up. They poured it into their hairy faces as fast as I could pour it into the cups!

And a drunk Viking is a vile Viking, I can tell you. For a bit of sport they dragged the old Archbishop of Canterbury, Aelfheah, into the hall. He's been their prisoner for seven months. They started shouting at him, 'How much are you going to pay to set yourself free, you snotty Saxon?' (At least that's what Agnes said they said.)

The old arch-bish was so calm! He just said, 'Nothing. And I will not allow the king or my church to pay you anything! The poor should not have to pay taxes to set me free.'

Well, that drove the Vikings mad as a nest of vipers. One of the Viking warriors took his sword out and raised it over the old bloke's head. 'No silver, no Saxon!' he cried.

'Wait!' the Viking leader roared. 'You cannot spill the blood of a holy man. We'll be cursed!'

So the Viking warrior looked crafty and grinned a black-and-yellow-toothed grin. He picked up an ox bone from the feast and threw it at the old arch-bish. It cracked the old guy right on the conk and he fell. 'See! No blood!' the warrior laughed.

That gave them all the idea for a bit of sport! Every Viking picked up a bone and pelted the old man — some of them even threw ox heads at him that had been picked clean. The bish took it bravely for a while — then he fell. Only one brave Viking tried to stop them but they ignored him.

At last their leader walked up to the half-dead arch-bish. Aelfheah had converted him to Christianity just the day before so I expected him to help the bish! Huh! No chance. He simply smacked him with the blunt side of his axe to finish him off.

Then they went back to their drinking till they drank themselves senseless. When they were all snoring we had to drag the old man out of the feasting hall and me and Agnes took him to the local church.

I am absolutely shattered. Working all night, dragging bodies all morning. I tell you, Mum. If you see those Vikings heading for your house then run. And pray they don't find the bones our dog buried in the garden. Your loving daughter, Hilda

Aelfheah's death was remembered and a church built on the spot where he died. It's still there in Greenwich today while his body was taken back to Canterbury.

He was made a Saxon saint … and probably deserved it!

Eth's death, then Ed's dead

Here's a totally useless bit of information for you to impress your teacher with:

In 1013 Viking king Swein arrived. (Rearrange the letters to make 'Swine' ... which the Saxons must have called him!) Eth ran away to Normandy so the Vikings couldn't kill him.

Swein died in 1014. The Vikings wanted their Cnut to rule. But the Saxons welcomed back Ethelred ... so long as he promised to be a better ruler. Then in 1016 he died. A really mean Victorian historian sneered ...

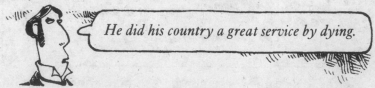

Eth's son, Edmund, gave Viking Cnut a few beatings in battle and they split the country between them, the way Alfred had – Danes in the north and east, Saxons in the south and west. It may have stayed like that but Ed did a really stupid thing – as daft as his dad Eth – he went and died! Cnut took over the whole country and Saxon rule was finished for 25 years.

How to be a Great king

Cnut may have been a Viking but a lot of historians think he was a 'good' king. He was named Cnut the Great. But we horrible historians know better. You don't get to be 'Great' without splattering blood around like water at a swimming gala.

Cnut was a Viking and he was a bad loser. He took Saxon hostages in East Anglia. When he was attacked by the Saxons he set sail into the English Channel. Cruel Cnut dropped the hostages off in Kent – but only after he'd dropped their hands and noses off into the sea.

Cnut was worried that Edmund's brothers would take over dead Ed's claim to the throne. He had Eadwig murdered.

To stop Edmund's step-bothers Edward and Alfred claiming dead Ed's throne he married their mother – if they fought him they'd have to fight their mum! Neither boy fancied that so they fled. Cnut was not bothered by the fact he already had a girlfriend and two sons (Swein and Harald) up in Northampton.

There were some English leaders that Cnut didn't trust. They had promised to obey him, but he wasn't sure. Just to be on the safe side he executed them. Earl Uhtred of Northumbria, for example, went to make peace with Cnut. Uhtred's own treacherous servant, Wighill, ran out from a hiding place and murdered him. It seems Cnut gave Wighill the order.

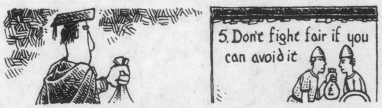

Cnut won a lot of battles. But he often cheated. When he attacked Norway in 1028 he sent large amounts of English money to princes so they would betray their king. Cnut conquered Norway with wallets for weapons.

Cnut couldn't beat Edmund in the war for the English throne, until Ed was betrayed by Mercian lord Eadric. Cnut made peace with Edmund and they swore to be 'brothers' ... and a few months later Edmund conveniently died. Surely Cnut the 'Great' wouldn't arrange to have a noble 'brother' bumped off!?! What do you think?

He was a tough nut (and a tough Cnut), but he was a 'Great' king – wasn't he?

Saxon crime and punishment

The Saxons certainly didn't mess about if you broke one of their laws.

King Edmund became an English saint – a good Christian who was captured by Viking bullies and chose to die horribly rather than give up his religion. You may be starting to feel sorry for Ed. DON'T!

Ed was not a kind and gentle king. Look at how he treated runaway slaves. (Slaves were known to the Saxons as 'thralls'.)

Grave for slaves

By the decree of King Edmund

WANTED

DEAD OR ALIVE

Thralls who have abandoned their masters and turned outlaw.
These men and women must be hunted and captured. Then an example must be made of those captured as follows:

Leaders – to be hanged in public
Other runaways – to be flogged three times, scalped and their little fingers removed before being returned to work

Painful punishment

In pagan Saxon times crimes were avenged by 'feuds' where people took the law into their own hands – you know, the sort of thing that still goes on in classrooms today ...

The trouble is feuds could go on and on, maybe getting senseless and violent ...

...and not even death stopped the feud ...

So kings tried to replace revenge with payment …

Even a human life could have a price on it – a 'weregild'. If a person were killed then the killer would have to make a weregild payment to the victim's family. The richer you were the higher your weregild was. A dead lord's family would get more than a dead peasant's family would from the killer.

Even bits of your body had a price on them!

What's your nose worth compared to your toes? Can you match the body bit to the money?

Answers: 1d); 2a); 3e); 4b); 5c).

106

Whips and lips

Traitors, outlaws, witches, wizards and frequent thieves could all receive the death penalty. But the execution method varied from place to place, time to time and crime to crime. If you were caught, how would you like to go? Which of these Saxon punishments would you choose to suffer?

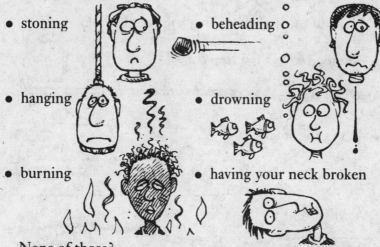

- stoning
- beheading
- hanging
- drowning
- burning
- having your neck broken

None of those?

All right. A merciful Saxon judge may teach you a lesson with a bit of mutilation – that is, he'd have bits cut off you. Which could you do without … ?

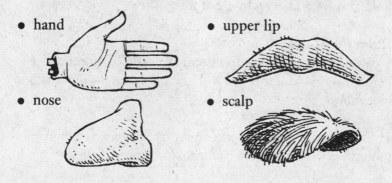

- hand
- upper lip
- nose
- scalp

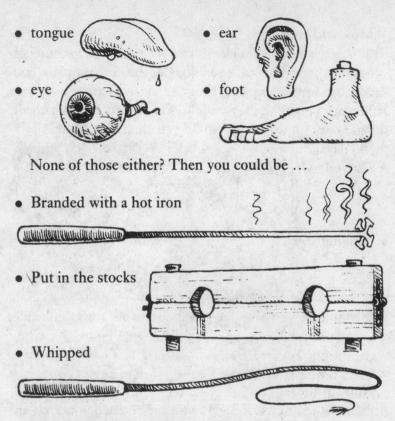

- tongue
- ear
- eye
- foot

None of those either? Then you could be ...

- Branded with a hot iron

- Put in the stocks

- Whipped

You'd rather go to prison?

Sorry – there may be a cellar in the lord's manor house to hold you for a short while, but no prisons.

Judgement day

Saxons held their trials in assemblies called folk moots. Try being a judge at a folk moot. How many can you get right, your honour?

1 Sanctuary Geraint the goat thief has reached the monastery church where he claims 'sanctuary' – that is to say your law officers can't enter the church and take him off to jail. But if every criminal runs to the abbey then the place would be full of thieves and killers. So a time limit has to be put on the sanctuary. How long will you let a criminal stay in sanctuary before you send the lads in to drag him out?

a) 40 hours.

b) 40 days.

c) 40 years.

2 Thieves Some criminals like Cuthwine never learn. He has been caught stealing and you have fined him. Now he's been caught again. How are you, his Saxon judge, going to punish him this time for repeated stealing?

a) Cut off his hair.

b) Cut off his hand.

c) Cut off his head.

3 Child cruelty Some parents are accidentally cruel to their children because they try out 'cures' for illnesses without realizing the dangers. In the early 700s a law has been passed, as you know, your honour. It means you must sentence Brigit to five years of punishment if she does what to cure her daughter's fever?

a) Holds the child too close to the fire.

b) Ducks her in the village pond.

c) Puts her on the roof or puts her in the oven.

4 Foreigners Foreigners in Saxon England can't be trusted because they might be spies for an enemy. So a foreigner must stay on the main roads and tracks, and if he leaves the path he has to let everyone know by blowing a horn or shouting. Maelgwn has been arrested for breaking this law. What must you do to him, your honour?

a) Put him to death as a thief.

b) Send him back to his own country.

c) Fine him a penny for every step he took off the path.

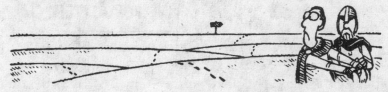

5 Fines There were no prisons in your local Saxon villages. Fines were easier to arrange. Which of these crimes must you punish with a fine, your honour?

a) Eating meat on a 'fast' or holy day.

b) Making a sacrifice to a pagan god.

c) Unlawful marriage.

IT'S MY FIRST FAST FEAST FINE!

6 Manslaughter Murder is not seen as a crime against the victim, but a crime against the victim's family. So, if a man is killed his family suffer because he is no longer there to earn a living for them. The family will demand his 'weregild' – his value in cash. But Benedict killed Alwin accidentally when a tree he was cutting fell on his neighbour. What must you order Benedict to do, your honour?

a) Pay the family the weregild money the same as for a murder.

b) Take the place of the victim in the family.

c) Kill himself.

7 Trials Edwin is suspected of stealing a pig. You ordered him to come to the village for a trial. (If Edwin doesn't turn up then he is 'Guilty'.) You have no police force to collect evidence – and no fingerprints to prove that a criminal was there. How can you check a suspect's story?

a) If he swears an oath on the Bible you must believe every word he says.

b) If he remains silent you must decide he is innocent.

c) If he swears an oath but stumbles over words (or stammers) you take it as a sign he is guilty.

8 Ordeals Egbert says he is innocent and wants to take a trial by 'ordeal' – a dangerous test in which God will protect him if he is innocent. What 'ordeal' will you allow Egbert to take?

a) He must grip a red-hot iron bar … and not be burned.

b) He must be tied up and thrown in the river … and float.

c) He must pull a stone from a pot of boiling water … and not be scalded.

9 Punishments Your court has found Theodoric guilty of witchcraft. You may choose to hang him. Which of these three other execution methods could you use in Saxon England, your honour?

a) Boiling.

b) Starving.

c) Guillotine.

10 Outlaws Cormac is a criminal who has run away from your punishment, then lived outside the law – he is declared an 'outlaw'. This means …

a) He doesn't have to pay taxes.

b) He is not allowed to go to church.

c) Anyone can kill him without having to stand trial for his murder.

Answers:

1b) Sanctuary lasted 40 days. But you only got 40 days if you handed over your weapons. If the criminal hadn't escaped in those 40 days he was taken to court and tried. Criminals could also claim sanctuary in a royal household! (They couldn't be throne out!) The trouble is someone has to sit outside the church for forty days to make sure he doesn't escape. Talk about crimewatch.

2b) A criminal could have his hand cut off, especially someone who stole from a church. Another common punishment was to 'brand' a criminal – burn a mark on his skin – so that everyone could see what he'd been up to and take extra care of their belongings when he was around.

3c) The writer of the law claimed that women put their daughters on the roof or in the oven to cure a fever! Do NOT let your mother read this book in case she gets some sad Saxon idea into her head and pops you in to bake.

4a) Very harsh, but in the days when very few people left their own village strangers were seen as dangerous. Even a great teacher and preacher like Bede never went further than a hundred miles north or south of his home monastery. Nowadays we're more trusting of strangers – even if they come from Clacton-on-Sea!

5a), b) and c) These were *all* fined.

6a) 'Blood money' had to be paid to the family of a victim, even if it was an accident.

7c) The accused could also call witnesses in his defence. Each witness would swear an oath that the accused was innocent. If enough witnesses took the oath *without a mistake* then that was also seen as a sign of innocence.

8 a), b) and c) *All* of these were Saxon tests of guilt. The hot iron bar must be carried one to three metres before being dropped. You can try this in class – you suspect Bertram Brown of pinching your pencil? See if he can carry a hot dog three metres without being burned!

9a) As well as boiling, burning was also a Saxon execution method.

10c) Outlaws did not have the protection of the law. Catch one and you could do whatever you liked with him – use him for target practice, get him to do your washing up or your homework or walk your pet rabbit. What would *you* use a captive outlaw for?

Did you know … ?

Not all of the early Saxon judges had been just or honest. They did favours for friends and filled their pockets with fines. King Alfred the Great made the Saxon courts much fairer. He sorted out the cheating judges and replaced them with honest ones. What happened to the dishonest judges? Alfred had them hanged. They didn't do as much cheating after that.

Not-so-sweet sixteen

If you committed a crime you were punished, whatever your age … until King Athelstan came along. One case changed Athelstan's mind and changed the law. If there had been a Saxon newspaper in the Dark Ages then it may have broken the news like this …

BINGO   12 August 927

Saxon Times

STILL ONLY HALF A GROAT OR HALF A GOAT

KING'S KINDNESS TO KENT KID!

The people of Maidstone in Kent were cheated of their sport today by King Athelstan. The king got to hear of the case of sheep-rustling Edward Medway. We reported last week how the shepherd killed one of his own sheep and ate its leg. He said the sheep was killed by wolves but the leg had been neatly cut off and its throat slit. As the Maidstone magistrate said, 'I've never seen a wolf that carries a knife!'

The magistrate then sentenced the sheep-slasher to hang by the neck, today at noon. Crowds had gathered from around the county and a fair had been set up in the square around the gallows. Then came the sensational news! King Athelstan has changed the law so crafty criminals like evil Ed can't be killed!

The king wrote to Bishop Theodred and said, 'It is not fair that a man should die so young. Or for such a small offence when he has seen others get away with it elsewhere.' The new law says that no one can be executed if they are under sixteen years of age.

Edward Medway, of course, is twelve years old. But the *Saxon Times* says, 'If he's old enough to steal a sheep he's old enough to swing for it!' We'll soon have fourteen- and fifteen-year-olds getting away with murder!

The only killer kids who can be executed are those that try to fight their way out of being arrested or who run away. Sadly Ed Med did not try to fight or run so the Maidstone holiday crowds went home disappointed.

No hanging today!

Of course there wasn't a Saxon newspaper – there weren't enough people who could read. But the tale of the hungry shepherd is true and shows just how desperate some people could get.

Vile verse

The Saxons had no television. (Even if they had, it would have been useless because they had no electricity to switch it on.) So they entertained themselves with riddles and long stories to pass the long winter nights.

Rotten riddles

One of the most popular pastimes was creating 'riddles' for friends to solve. A riddle was usually told as if it was an object 'speaking' ...

Q: I hang between sky and earth; I grow hot from fires and bubble like a whirlpool. What am I?

A: A cooking pot hanging over a fire.

Children did it, adults did it and even the monks did it. Here are some more Saxon riddles ...

Q: On the way to a miracle water becomes bone.

A: Ice.

Q: I watched four fair creatures
Travelling together; they left black tracks
behind them. The support of the bird
moved swiftly; it flew in the sky,
dived under the waves.

A: Four fingers and a quill pen.

Q: I am told a certain object grows
In the corner, rises and expands, throws up
a crust. A proud wife carried off
the boneless wonder, the daughter of a king
covered that swollen thing with a cloth.

A: Bread.

Verse and worse

Since Saxons didn't have many books, and so few people could read, most of their stories had to be learned by heart. Now a storyteller can remember a story better if the tale is turned into a poem. Even bits of their history books were written in poetry when the writer got excited about it.

Monster munches

When King Athelstan defeated an army of invading Irish with their savage Scots friends, the Saxons success was recorded in the *Anglo-Saxon Chronicle*. This would be one of the good bits, like the good but gruesome bits you like to hear in your favourite fairy tales – you know the sort of thing: 'Ooooh Grandmama! What big eyes you have!' 'All the better to smell you with.'

Imagine those manic monks sitting round the fire and listening to this part ...

The field grew dark with the soldiers' blood
And the corpses were left behind.
The bodies they left to be shared by the beasts
Like the ravens in dusty black coats.
And the grey-coated eagle, the greedy war hawk,
The great grey-haired beast of the forest.

You could try reciting that to someone you don't like, just as they are about to tuck into their school dinner!

As you can see, Saxon poems didn't actually rhyme though. Maybe we can ruin a couple by changing a few words around and making them rhyme ...

Crime story

Today we read crime stories in books and newspapers and we watch them in films or on television. The Saxons' main entertainment was listening to story-poems, so it's not surprising there were crime stories in their poetry. But, being Saxons, the stories were so horrible they'd be given an '18' certificate in the cinema today. You would not want to read such horror, so don't read this updated Saxon poem extract below ...

The Fates of Men

And now he's dead we've hung him up
Upon a roadside gibbet high.
For wicked crimes such men as this
Deserve to suffer and to die.
Such evil men should not live on,
My friends, you must not groan or cry.
See how his helpless hands cannot
Drive off the crows that peck his eyes.

Little Alfie's eyes

Then there was the murder of Prince Alfred in 1036. Poor little Alfie just wanted to be king after the Danish King Cnut died. But Earl Godwin, Saxon Earl of Wessex, had other ideas. This poem based on the *Anglo-Saxon Chronicle* report reveals all ...

Prince Alfred was a cheerful lad, with eyes of sparkling blue,
Till Godwin had his eyes put out. Yes, both! Not one, but two!
He sent the blinded prince away to be a monk in Ely,
There the little Alfie died; did Godwin care? Not really.

Then Godwin set about the slaying of Alf's friends.
He had them caught and had them brought to really sticky ends.
Some he sold as slaves for cash and some he scalped their heads,
Others he locked up in chains and some he killed stone dead.

Some he had their hands chopped off or arms or legs or ears.
No wonder they all fled (or tried to flee) in fear.
We've never seen a crueller deed been done in all our land
Since those dread Vikings came and took peace from our hands.

The Saxons believed that God took revenge on evil doers. 'An eye for an eye', the Bible said. So they would be pleased to know that Godwin's son, Harold, died at the battle of Hastings 30 years later … with an arrow in his eye! And that was the end of the gruesome Godwins.

Pester your parents

Your parents probably went to school in the days when history was planned to send them to sleep. So they won't know these fascinating facts, the odd things that make history interesting.

Find a parent – you'll probably find one stuck in front of a television – and say, 'Dearest parent, will you either give me ten pounds pocket money or help me with my history homework?' When they say, 'Homework!' then you've got them! Ask these fiendish questions ...

1 In England in the 700s what were Noxgagas and Ohtgagas?
a) Instruments of torture that cut off noses and naughty bits.
b) Tribes of people.
c) The Saxon names for carrots and cabbages (or maybe cabbages and carrots).

2 The bitchy monk Alcuin complained to King Offa: 'Some idiot thinks up a new-fangled idea and the next minute the whole country is trying to copy it!' What was he talking about?
a) A new fashion for playing football.
b) A new fashion for a sort of bunjee-jumping with leather ropes.
c) A new fashion for fancy clothes.

3 In 975 King Edgar died suddenly, the harvest was poor and the Saxons starved. What was blamed?
a) A comet appearing in the skies.
b) King Ed walking under a ladder.
c) People not going to church every Sunday.

4 The Britons tried to attack Saxon Athelfrith around AD 603 but were wiped out. What nickname did they give this cunning fighter?
a) The Twister.
b) The Twirler.
c) The Twerp.

WHIZZ ZZ LOP!

HE MIGHT *FIGHT* LIKE A TWIRLER BUT HE *LOOKS* LIKE A TWERP

5 An assassin stabbed King Edwin of Northumbria with a long dagger. The dagger had to pass through something else first and that saved Edwin. What did the dagger pass through?
a) The wall of the tent where Edwin was sleeping.
b) A Bible that Edwin was carrying.
c) One of Edwin's soldiers.

6 Two cruel young monks discovered the historian Bede was almost blind and played a trick on him. What?
a) They took Bede out to a dangerous cliff, then ran off and left him to find his own way home – or fall off the cliff.
b) They told Bede there was a church full of monks waiting

to hear him preach and led him there. He preached, but the church was empty.

c) They pretended to read a letter to Bede that said his brother was dead, run over by a mad horse.

7 In 1006 a Scottish army was defeated at Durham. The Scots' heads were cut off and stuck on poles around the castle walls. Durham women offered to do what for the relatives of the dead heads?

a) Wash the heads' faces and comb their hair so they looked nice.

b) Act as scarecrows to stop birds pecking the heads.

c) Chase away the children who were throwing wooden balls at the heads and trying to knock them off .

8 Saxon King Ethelred was plagued by Viking raids. He came up with a way of dealing with his problems. What?

a) He had Viking leaders killed.

b) He had Viking women killed.

c) He had Saxon leaders killed.

9 There was no Saxon soap powder. They made their own detergent from ashes, animal fat and ...

a) snot.

b) pee.

c) spit.

10 In 686 the villagers of Jarrow went to the local monastery and brought death to the monks. How?

a) The villagers had the plague.

b) The 'villagers' were really Viking warriors in disguise.

c) The villagers came to muck out the stables, upset a lantern in the straw and burned the monastery to the ground while the monks slept and roasted.

Answers:

1b) These people were part of the Mercian kingdom and lived south of the River Thames. Sadly their names have been forgotten in most histories, along with the Wixnas and Wigestas, the Hurstingas and the Feppingas. And you can no longer call yourself (proudly) a Hicca or a Gifla! The West Willas went with the Wigesta, the Wideringas ... and the wind.

2c) The miserable monk thought everyone should wear plain, boring clothes (like history teachers do today). But kings, queens and their courtiers liked flashy, colourful clothes with brooches and embroidery like Dark Age pop stars. Alcuin wore a habit in a delightful shade of mud brown with a smart rope belt and did not approve of painted posers.

3a) If a comet appeared in the sky it was a sure sign of disaster. One appeared in 1066 and, sure enough, the Saxon kingdom was conquered for good.

4a) Athelfrith was known as the Twister, probably because of the way he whirled his sword and not because he ran a fairground ride in his spare time. In a battle against the Welsh some British monks prayed for the Welsh to win. 'Twister' Athelfrith was upset and butchered the 1,200 unarmed monks before going on to massacre the Welsh.

5c) The assassin, Eumer, said he had a message for Edwin. He came up to the king and drew his dagger. One of Edwin's lords, Lilla, threw himself in front of the king. Eumer's powerful thrust went clean through Lilla and wounded the king. Another lord died before the assassin was finally hacked to death.

6b) Bede (so the story goes) was led to the empty church and began preaching to the empty seats while the two young monks laughed themselves sick. But Bede had the last laugh because the church filled up with angels who came down from heaven to hear the old guy.

7a) The women offered to comb the hair of the dead Scots, but they wanted to be well paid for this – a bit like hairdressers today really.

8c) Ethelred trusted no one. In 1006 he had his Saxon leader in York murdered because he was afraid the man was becoming too powerful. Just to be extra sure he took the man's sons and had their eyes put out.

9b) It's supposed to work but don't try this at home. If human pee is such a good cleaner then how come babies nappies are so disgusting when they're full of the stuff?

10a) Most people think of the plague as arriving with the Black Death in 1349, but there were deadly diseases long before that. When the sickness reached Jarrow the villagers flocked to the monastery to get the herbs and cures the monks made. The villagers died and the monks caught the plague from them. Only two monks survived. So much for helping your neighbours!

Epilogue

You can blame the Saxons for a lot.

The monk Bede practically invented English history. Other writers had written about events in the past but Bede sorted them out into some sort of order and gave them dates. As a result history teachers have something to test you on.

Bede would be delighted that we still follow his system.

You can blame him for the Millennium, by the way. Bede sorted out the calendar for you. People used to work out the year by the reign of the monarch ... so the year 2000, say, would have been 'the 47th year of Elizabeth II's reign'. Bede preferred to work time out from the date of the birth of Jesus. So he did. And we still do. Bede would be proud.

And, of course, Bede said the world was round when everyone else thought it was flat. And some sad people (like geography teachers and science teachers) still believe that round-earth nonsense when sensible people like you can see quite plainly that it isn't! But Bede would be pleased.

Then there was the Saxon King Alfred. He reckoned that the Saxons suffered Viking attacks because they had behaved badly. Viking raids were God's punishment. He said the only way for people to be better was to learn more – and people still believe it, so Alfred is partly to blame for you having to go to school and he'd be burning cakes with happiness to see you suffering there!

Athelstan was the first king to make the whole of Britain one country, and it still is – until those Scots in the north get their independence. Athelstan would be chuffed.

Of course the nasty Normans came along and the sad Saxons were defeated. But the Saxon language lived on – which is why you're reading this book in a sort of Saxon English and not Norman French.

King Offa would be pleased at that.

So, thank you Offa, Alfred, Athelstan, and Bede – but a special thanks to those ordinary Saxons whose names never went down in history books. You struggled and died, and made life better for those who came after you.

Smashing Saxons every one.